T0342776

Zoom Out!

by Ben Hubbard

OXFORD
UNIVERSITY PRESS
AUSTRALIA & NEW ZEALAND

OXFORD
UNIVERSITY PRESS

Oxford University Press is a department of the University
of Oxford. It furthers the University's objective of excellence in
research, scholarship, and education by publishing worldwide.
Oxford is a registered trademark of Oxford University Press in
the UK and in certain other countries.

Published in Australia by Oxford University Press
Level 8, 737 Bourke Street, Docklands, Victoria 3008, Australia

Text © Ben Hubbard 2014, 2019

The moral rights of the author have been asserted

First published 2014
This edition 2019
Reprinted 2021

All rights reserved. No part of this publication may be reproduced,
stored in a retrieval system, or transmitted, in any form or by
any means, without the prior permission in writing of Oxford
University Press, or as expressly permitted by law, by licence, or
under terms agreed with the reprographics rights organisation.
Enquiries concerning reproduction outside the scope of the above
should be sent to the Rights Department, Oxford University Press,
at the address above.

You must not circulate this work in any other form and you must
impose this same condition on any acquirer.

ISBN 9780190316891

Series Editor: Nikki Gamble
Printed in Singapore by Markono Print Media Pte Ltd
*Links to third party websites are provided by Oxford in good faith and
for information only. Oxford disclaims any responsibility for the materials
contained in any third party website referenced in this work.*

Acknowledgements

The publishers would like to thank the following for the
permission to reproduce photographs:

p1: Corbis/ESA/Hubble Collaboration/Handout/CNP; **p2–3**: Corbis/
Ugo Mellone/SOPA RF; **p4–5**: Science Photo Library/Louise Hughes;
p5b: Alamy/Mark Eveleigh, Getty Images/Antagain; **p6–7**: Alamy/
Mark Eveleigh, Getty Images/Antagain; **p7t**: Nature Picture Library/
Warwick Sloss; **p7b**: Getty Images/Danita Delimont; **p8**: Nature
Picture Library/Andy Rouse; **p8–9**: Getty Images/Danita Delimont;
p9b: Beverly Joubert/Getty Images; **p10–11**: Beverly Joubert/Getty
Images; **p10t**: Mogens Trolle/Shutterstock; **p10b**: Maggy Meyer/
Shutterstock; **p11t**: Corbis/DLILLC; **p11b**: Getty Images/UIG; **p12**:
Getty Images/UIG; **p13t**: Eugene Kalenkovich/Shutterstock; **p13b**:
Getty Images/alxpin; **p14–15**: Getty Images/alxpin; **p15**: Getty
Images/alxpin; **p16**: Corbis/ESA/Hubble Collaboration/Handout/CNP

Cover photographs by Baris Simsek/Getty Images & Srdjan111/
Shutterstock; Corbis/ESA/Hubble Collaboration/Handout/CNP

We have made every effort to trace and contact all copyright
holders before publication. If notified, the publisher will rectify
any errors or omissions at the earliest opportunity.

Contents

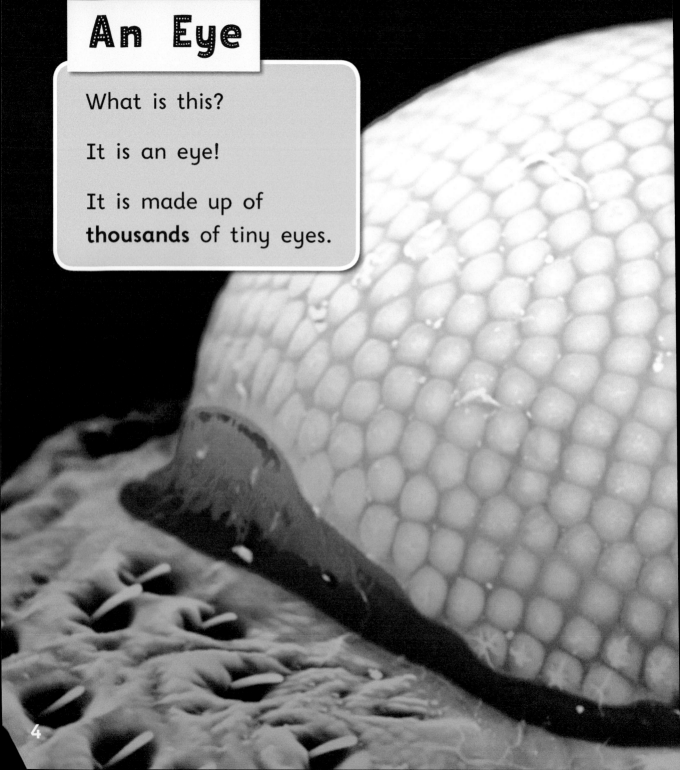

An Eye

What is this?

It is an eye!

It is made up of **thousands** of tiny eyes.

4

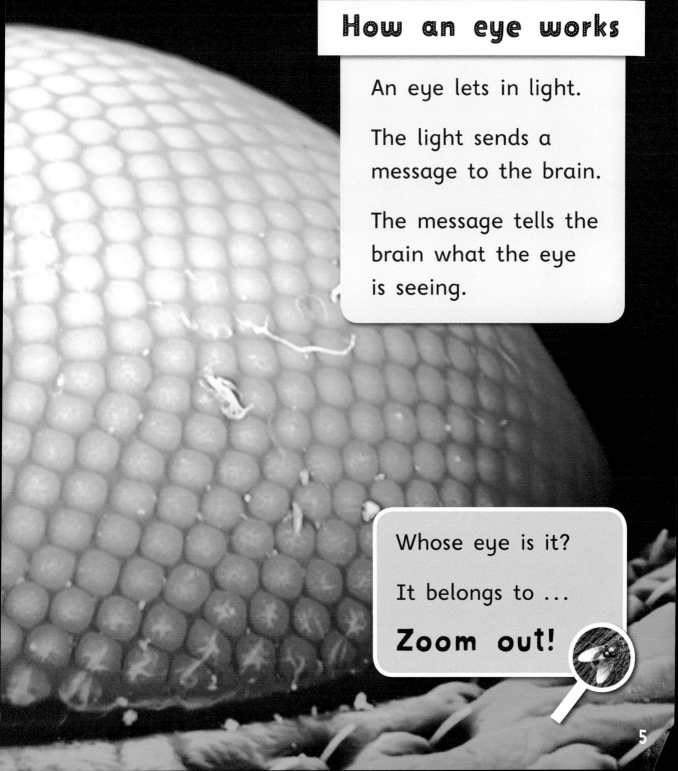

How an eye works

An eye lets in light.

The light sends a message to the brain.

The message tells the brain what the eye is seeing.

Whose eye is it?

It belongs to ...

Zoom out!

A Fly

A fly has two buzzing wings and six sticky feet.

This means it can land anywhere – and on anything.

How flies eat

Did you know that flies taste with their feet?

But they can't eat solid food.

They have to spit on food to make it liquid.

Then they suck up the liquid food. Their mouths are shaped like straws!

Where has this fly landed?

It has landed on ...

Zoom out!

An Elephant

Elephants are the largest animals on land.

They have thick, wrinkled skin.

Elephants spray their skin with mud. This keeps them cool in the sun.

Elephant herds

A family of elephants is called a **herd**.

A mother elephant leads the herd from place to place.

The herd is looking for shade, water and food.

Where is this elephant?

It is in ...

Zoom out!

Kenya

Kenya is a hot country.

It has many amazing wild animals.

As well as elephants, there are animals like rhinos, zebras and lions.

Kenya also has more than 1000 different kinds of birds.

Kenyan people

Some Kenyan people live in big, busy cities. Others, like the **Masai** people, live on the **plains**.

Some animals from the plains are dangerous – such as lions and leopards.

There are fences around the Masai villages to keep out dangerous animals.

Where is Kenya?

It is in ...

Zoom out!

Africa

The **continent** of Africa is very big and very hot.

It has **deserts**, plains, mountains and forests. There are 54 different countries in Africa.

Over one **billion** people live there.

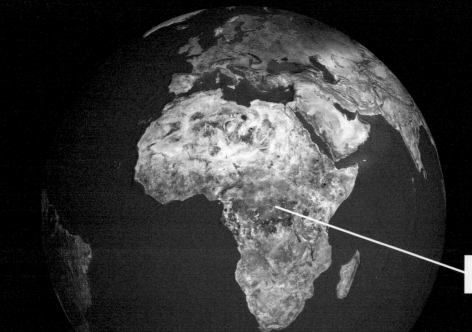

Africa

Land and sea

Africa is the second biggest continent in the world.

There are seven continents in total.

A continent is an area of land where we live.

However, most of the world is sea.

Where is Africa?

It is on ...

Zoom out!

Earth

Our world is the **planet** Earth.

From space, all of the sea makes Earth look blue.

Earth is one of the eight planets in the **solar system**.

Together, these planets circle around the sun.

Earth

If you zoomed out more, the solar system would seem small.

The planets would look tiny – like the eyes of a fly!

You could keep zooming out from the solar system.

Then you would go further out into the **universe**.

You could go on zooming out forever.

You would never reach the end.

Glossary

billion: one thousand million (1 000 000 000)

continent: a huge area of land that can include many countries

deserts: areas of land where it hardly ever rains and there are not many plants

herd: a group of animals

Masai: a tribal people who live in Kenya and Tanzania

plains: large areas of flat countryside without many trees

planet: a large ball of rock or gas that revolves around a star

solar system: a sun and the planets that revolve around it

thousands: numbers such as 3000 and 6000

universe: the stars, the planets and everything that exists

Index